Cats In Space
Coloring Book

Helpful Tips for Coloring

★ There are many tools for coloring: crayons, markers, fine tip pens, pastels, etc. Experiment with what works best for your style and designs. You can even mix coloring mediums on an image. Think outside of the box!

★ Sometimes colors appear differently than you expect. The color test page is a great way to try out your colors and shading beforehand.

★ When using colored pencils, be sure to keep them sharp. This will help when coloring smaller areas or fine details.

★ If using markers or pens, be sure to put a scrap piece of paper behind the page you are coloring. This will help prevent color bleeding onto the next page.

★ When using pencils, pastels or crayons, start out light. You can always go back and darken your colors.

★ Start on an image wherever you feel comfortable. There is no "wrong" place to begin. If you get overwhelmed or discouraged by an image, take a break and come back to it later.

★ Remember to practice. The more you do it, the more comfortable it will become....but there is no perfect, just your creativity, enjoyment and relaxation!

COLOR TEST PAGE

COLOR TEST PAGE

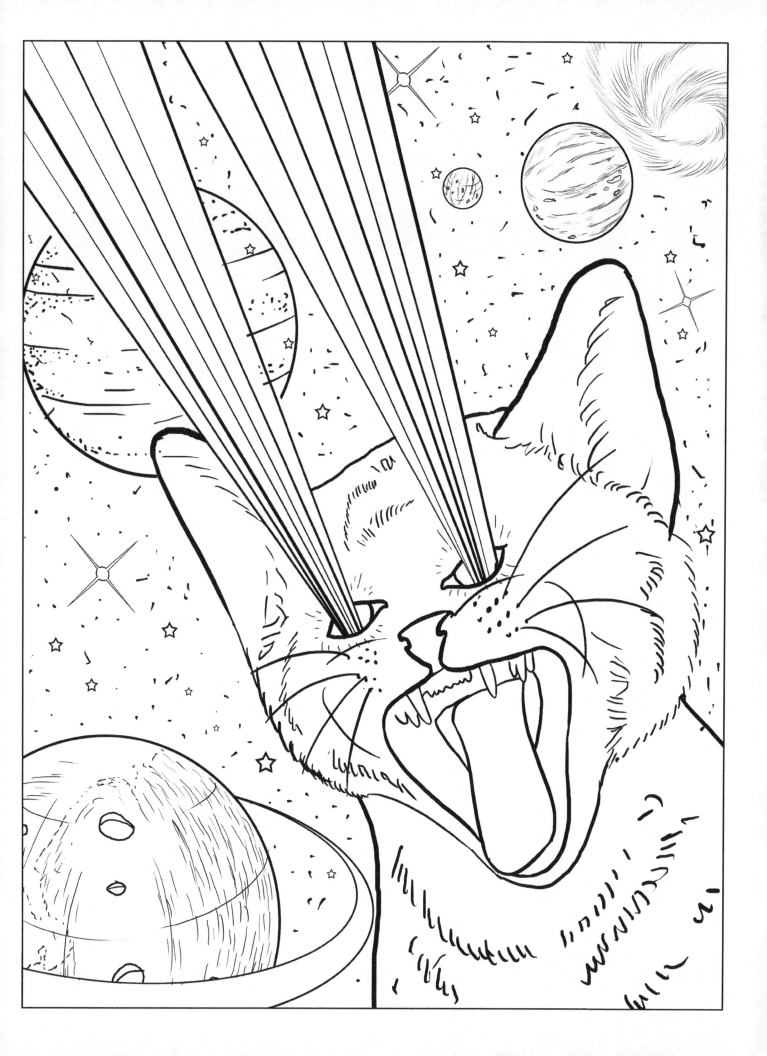

Made in the USA
Middletown, DE
16 December 2018